THE DEVELOPMENT OF SCIENCE AMONG NATIONS

JULIUS FREIHERR VON LIEBIG

The superiority of man to animals essentially consists in his power of making inventions which tend to satisfy his necessities ; the amount of these inventions amongst a people determines its degree of civilisation.

Nielrow Editions

Dijon – France

Portrait de Liebig : BIUsante - Paris

ISBN : 978-2-490446-14-8

JUSTUS FREIHERR VON LIEBIG
(1803-1873)
ENGREAVING – 1843 – ERNST RAUCH
FROM A PAINTING BY WILHELM TRAUTSCHOLD

THE DEVELOPMENT OF SCIENCE AMONG NATION

BY

**BARON JUSTUS LIEBIG – F. R. S.
PRESIDENT OF THE ROYAL ACADEMY OF
SCIENCES AT MÜNICH
MEMBER OF THE FRENCH INSTITUTE
ETC.**

**EDINBURGH
EDMONTON AND DOUGLAS**

1867

EDINBURGH : T. CONSTABLE,
PRINTER TO THE QUEEN, AND TO THE UNIVERSITY.

THE DEVELOPMENT OF SCIENCE AMONG NATIONS.

We are taught by the history of Science that our knowledge of bodies and phenomena has its origin in the material and mental requirements of men, and that its condition depends upon the state of progress which these have attained.

Unassisted by art, man is unable to resist the outward injuries which continually endanger his existence, and the active pressure of the external world challenges his dormant mental powers to combat these hostile influences.

Everything that he needs as a protection against climate and weather, and against his enemies, or that he may require for his subsistence or restoration to health, is derived from Nature, which thus communicates to him a knowledge of countless objects and their peculiarities, of the action of fire, and many processes by which he adapts the raw material to the purposes of life.

In a former treatise I drew attention to the peculiar power possessed by the imagination of connecting together the pictures conjured up by the impressions of the senses, and of drawing conclusions from them. The inferences thus drawn are related to each other in the same way as ideas brought into unison by the understanding ; but have this difference, that the conclusions of the imagination are only pictures. An impression of the senses stands in the same relation to the imagination as a word does to the understanding when it acts as the symbol of a thought.

The *word* « tar » has not necessarily any effect on the imagination of most men, while the smell of it may conjure up the picture of a vessel, or of a sea-shore which had been visited years before.

The agriculturist, the herdsman, and the hunter are in immediate communication with nature. The first learns by the simple perceptions of his senses how sunshine and rain affect the growth of plants ; how a seed germinates and develops itself into a tree, how it blossoms and bears fruit. In the same way, the herdsman gathers much experience as to the nourishment and propagation of the animals under his protection ; he acquires familiarity with the diseases to which they are subject, and through these, with nutritive and poisonous herbs. By observing the firmament, he gains a knowledge of time by the course of the stars, and learns how they progress with the different seasons.

The priest who cuts up the sacrifices becomes acquainted with the intestines of animals, and of their mutual connexions. A number of such facts enable those who observe them to arrive at conclusions regarding the existence of other facts of a like kind.

The shepherd seeks for medicinal herbs for his sheep, and applies them to the use of man. From the changes produced by diseases in the organs of animals, the priest draws inferences in regard to the nature of human maladies. Thus the shepherd becomes the first therapeutist, and the priest the first pathologist.

The manufactures of soap, leather, glass, wine, oil, bread, and cheese resulted from inductions of a similar kind ; they are very old, as are also the employment of wool and flax in weaving, and the art of dyeing. The processes of extracting metals from their ores, such as copper, tin, and lead, and of using gold and silver, likewise belong to antiquity.

The superiority of man to animals essentially consists in his power of making inventions which tend to satisfy his necessities ; the amount of these inventions amongst a people determines its degree of civilisation.

The inventions of man in trades, manufactures, medicine, mechanics, and astronomy, supply the knowledge of facts, which at a later period become indispensable to the development of science ; for they lead to an acquaintance with the phenomena of motion, both in the heavens and on the surface of the earth, and they draw attention to the constituent parts of mineral bodies, as well as to those of plants and animals. But while practical art, founded on experiment, leads to such inventions, it does not of itself seek to disclose the character and first principles, either of bodies or of natural phenomena, because these lie quite beyond its practical aims.

The scientific knowledge of nature originates in a higher impulse, for it springs out of the intellectual necessities of man, as his mind compels him to give an account of the world in which he lives, and of the objects and phenomena coming daily under his observation. But in the beginning of his inquiries, man knows nothing of the nature of his senses, and is ignorant that the true or real nature of things is inaccessible to them. The senses should assist him to understand the external world, but they are to him, at this stage of his development, tools whose management he does not understand.

He sees and hears, yet he knows nothing of light or sound, and is ignorant whether visual rays pass out of his eyes or are received into them ; nor is he aware whether the temperature he feels is that of his own body.

History teaches us that the ideas of man upon objects and events in the external world have been developed in a similar way to that in which a child gradually learns to interpret the impressions of his senses. From the constant habit of using his hands, eyes, and tongue, the child learns to discriminate between form, colour, and quality. He ascertains through touch the resistance of solids as compared with liquids, the difference between heat and cold, dryness and damp ; then his further development chiefly depends on his ability to reproduce in himself the impressions received, without further help from the senses. Gradually well-defined pictures increase in his memory, and the human understanding begins unconsciously to propose questions to the senses. He compares and discovers resemblances and differences, - that cold under some circumstances can be converted into heat, that liquids may become solids and solids liquids ; but it is long before the characteristics of each object become known to him. Thus, for instance, the first idea of motion is attached to a hand which raises, pushes, or draws anything to itself.

Natural inquiry began with ideas of this kind, and its further general development advances as it would have done in an individual, with this difference, that the senses and understanding of many take part in it. Every one in handling objects, and in considering their relations to each other, views them from the position that he has attained. Of the object or phenomenon each person views a different aspect, one seeing it as it were in full face, another in profile, and thus by degrees all sides become equally known. At a later period, when details become more defined, it is discovered that many phenomena are complex, and that in their manifestation things co-operate which had formerly escaped the simple perceptive faculties. Man now loses his earlier confidence in the indications of the senses, and seeks for proofs to verify the impressions conveyed by them.

In this way there gradually arise fixed and limited ideas of bodies and of their actions, which become serviceable in forming rational conceptions of them, and with the increase of these the number of their combinations also grow. Reason now acquires dominion over the senses ; instead of vague questions to nature, there are now put definite inquiries, which multiply in their number and mere perceptions become changed into intelligent observations.

No one will assert that there could have existed during an earlier age any obstacles in the minds of men to prevent them from seeing and perceiving in the same way that we do now. Neither does the ground of difference between a former and later contemplation of many phenomena consist in a want of facts. It is true that we possess more facts than the ancients, but those which most abundantly surround the commonest phenomena, such as air and fire, evaporation and freezing, steam and rain, heat and cold, were as well known and observed by men thousands of years ago as they are now. Thus no one will believe that, before the discovery of oxygen, there could have been the slightest doubt as to the necessity of air for combustion and respiration, or for a strong current of air to produce a high degree of heat.

Our improved understanding is not caused by our senses being more acute, or by our having a higher mental capability, -for the great philosophers of antiquity who devoted themselves to these subjects arrived at conclusions on the nature of objects and phenomena which are admitted now to be unsurpassed.

The reason of our improvement is that we have become richer in conceptions. But our ideas as to bodies, or what is the same, our acquaintance with perceptible objects, their peculiarities and actions, are not an inheritance of our nature. This knowledge must be gained from experience, and becomes developed in the human mind, in a way quite different from the development in animals, whose faculties expand to the the limit assigned to them, without their own co-operation, and in consequence of the effect of natural laws.

All these ideas have arisen or have been derived through impressions upon our perceptive faculties ; but as the phenomena of nature are always complex, and are produced by means of bodies possessing distinct and unchangeable characters, it is obvious that the rational conception of a body, or of a phenomenon related to it, must include within itself all these characteristics.

It is evident that when a single property of a body is unknown, a certain number of phenomena which have to do with it, or which are dependent for their manifestation on this unknown property, cannot be intelligible to the understanding, and hence it results that instead of the correct conception being formed, there is another created by the imagination. Thus, twenty-five years ago, the properties communicated to oxygen by *ozonizing* it, through the agency of electricity, or by contact with moist phosphorus, were not included in the conception of the nature of oxygen, and it followed, as a natural consequence, that the discoverer ascribed the effects which he perceived to the production of a body similar to chlorine, that element possessing like properties.

We speak of carbon as a constituent part of plants and animal bodies, without necessarily thinking of diamonds, wood, charcoal, or soot ; and, in like manner, we talk of phosphorus and iodine, although they do not occur in a free or native state. These are abstract conceptions, which, when they are once firmly fixed on the mind, will in all cases, provided their characteristics have been properly perceived, awaken the idea of carbon, phosphorus, or iodine.

As natural phenomena are connected like the knots in a net, it will be found, in studying a single phenomenon, that it is made up of certain conditions dependent upon bodies with active properties, each having something in common with the other ; and as the number of these conditions or parts is limited and proportionately small, we succeed at last in forming intellectual images of them all.

This is the problem of science, and its advance depends on the increase of facts, though it does not stand in relation to their number, but to the amount of notions and the quantity of thinking materials derived from them. A thousand facts in themselves do not alter the progressive state of science, while one fact that has become comprehensible ultimately outweighs them all.

The scientific inquirer is always apt to mix up with his own observations some of the conceptions of his time, which are believed to be true by his generation, although they are not so. They form part of his method of thought ; and this renders his conclusions uncertain without his knowing the cause, and lengthens very much the road which he has to travel before he gains correct conceptions of the external world.

These remarks on the development of our ideas acquired by experience, may perhaps be of use in leading to a more correct appreciation of the different periods of knowledge about natural phenomena than has hitherto been attained.

As the explanation of a natural phenomenon is a logical process, the understanding is able to fix beforehand the logical conditions necessary for the explanation. Aristotle does this when he says -

« The road to philosophy is like that to all other science. The facts must first be collected, and their cause ascertained. We must not study a whole mass of facts at once, but each singly by itself, and then draw our conclusions ; when we possess the facts, it is then our business to establish their points of connexion.

« These facts are gained by the perceptions of the senses ; if these are incomplete, the knowledge which has been built upon them will be so also.

« We can have no general theoretical proposition except through induction, and we can only have inductive ideas through the perceptive faculties, for these take cognizance of single facts. »

These are the main principles of inquiry which the greatest sage of antiquity has left us ; they are of the same value now as they were two thousand years ago.

If we now compare his explanations of natural phenomena or theories with those of all the inquirers into the laws of nature who succeeded him up to the present time, we find that the same opinion has ever been held as to the necessity that the ideas should accord with the facts, or, rather, that the explanation should correspond with the logical laws. Still the later theories were always contradicting the earlier ones ; those which were at one time considered correct were at a later period recognised as false ; the subsequent interpretations were always contradicting the preceding ones, and this constant change of explanations continued for hundreds of years. It is therefore clear that the truth of the explanations of phenomena does not depend on the principles of logic alone.

The correct explanation of a phenomenon depends on the completeness of our conceptions derived from experience. Hence, when we study the ideas of Aristotle, and the inquirers who succeeded him, we discover why the most highly developed understanding and the most acute logic were unable by themselves to come to just conclusions.

At first the facts comprised in one conception are undefined, their number and their extent being unknown ; it naturally follows that the first interpretations cannot be either fixed or definite, but that they must alter in proportion as the facts become more known, and as the unknown facts which belonged to the same conception are discovered and included in it. The earlier explanations are only relatively false, and the later ones only relatively true ; because our conceptions of the objects have become wider, more defined, and sharper. This development of ideas occurs in regular succession.

No more-lately developed conception can precede an earlier one, or if it do it is useless, because it is wanting in substance. The later ideas are intimately bound up with those that preceded them. In their explanations of natural phenomena, the Greek philosophers, and the inquirers who followed them, give the extent and substance of their empirical ideas, and nothing more ; but they offer from this point of view an especial interest for the history of the development of science, as we acknowledge that it is to them we owe the first plans for the building up of our conceptions.

Aristotle distinguished solids from liquids and gases. All solid objects are to him varieties of earth ; he thinks that transparency has something to do with water; but language does not suffice to define the other variations in solid bodies, with regard to form, colour, and hardness. One can only determine what may be extracted out of a body, or what proceeds from it. A white stone exposed to fire yields chalk ; another white stone melts into glass ; a red stone yields iron ; another red stone, quicksilver ; a grey stone, tin ; a black stone, lead. « The essence of bodies, » says Aristotle, « consists in form. » HERE WE HAVE THE FIRST IDEA OF CHEMICAL ANALYSIS.

« Daily experience teaches that solid bodies cannot float in the air or in space unless they are held up by something ; therefore, as one sees the stars behind the moon, and the moon is nearer to the earth than the sun, these heavenly bodies, being solid, must be fastened to transparent rings or spheres, which move with them round the earth. »

« When a stone falls unchecked it moves with increasing rapidity towards the earth. As neither the senses nor the reason can possibly admit that the earth has any share in its fall, it is clear that there must be a natural impulse in the stone to return to the place pointed out to it by nature. » HERE IS THE ORIGIN

OF THE CONCEPTION OF GRAVITY OR THE FORCE OF ATTRACTION.

The ideas of the Greeks were completely in unison with their experience, and were so far correct, inasmuch as they could have no others. The conception of time, which forms part of the compound idea of velocity, was developed and taken up about fifteen hundred years after Aristotle. The Greeks did not possess watches or timepieces for short intervals.

In the beginning of natural inquiry the complicated phenomena of rain, of rainbows, of combustion and respiration, were all regarded as simple ones ; later it was discovered that the formation of clouds preceded rain ; that without the sun no rainbow could exist; and without air no respiration or combustion could take place. The part of the phenomenon latest found out is always considered as the cause of the whole. Thus the sun is the cause of the rainbow, and air is the cause of combustion and respiration, in the same sense as the course of the moon is the cause of tides.

Therefore the discovery and establishment of the various properties of water by Thales, those of air by Anaximenes, and those of fire by Heraclitus, are classed among the greatest discoveries, because these philosophers have thereby prepared the ground for all the future questions which are associated with the most important actions on the surface of the earth, and with the lives of men and animals. These questions still occupy us at the present day.

The subtle analysis of the words by the Grecian philosophers teaches us, with great exactness, the amount of ideas comprised in the words used by them in their operations of thought. Thus it might be useful to compare the meaning applied in different periods to one of these words, such as AIR, with the signification it has at the present time, in order to gain a clear notion of the state of empirical ideas in former times, and of the manner in which they were developed into rational conceptions.

The Greeks knew that the air in a bladder resists pressure, and that an inverted glass does not fill with water. Air was then viewed as an element next in lightness to fire, the levity of which was recognised by the ascent of smoke, but though so light, it was known to occupy space, and to offer resistance to pressure. Until the beginning of the sixteenth century, it was thought that air could be converted into water, but in the middle of that century this idea was renounced, upon the discovery that air contained water in the form of steam. In the year 1630, it was observed that air possesses weight ; and in 1643, the discovery was made that it presses upon all other objects on the surface of the earth with its own entire weight. In year 1647, it was ascertained that the invisible particles of air press also on each other, and are elastic ; hence, that the lower layers of air are more dense than the upper ones. In 1660 it was found that different kinds of air, elastic like common air, could be artificially produced by means of chemical pocesses ; and in 1727 that similar kinds of air exist in plants, animal matter, and calcareous minerals ; these kinds of air being shown to be educts, not products, some being combustible, others extinguishing fire. In 1774 further experiments elicited the fact that there existed a kind of air in which combustible bodies burn more briskly than in common air. It was further discovered, in 1775, that atmospheric air is principally composed of two kinds of air, the one supporting combustion, the other not ; and that it also contains a variable quantity of steam. Towards the end of the eighteenth century, carbonic acid was recognised as a constituent of air ; and in the nineteenth century ammonia and nitric acid were also found ; finally, it was discovered that many kinds of spores of fungi float in it.

Our present position, with regard to the conception of air, has been acquired by the work of hundreds of the most acute men, during a space of more than two thousand years, and by the continual enlargement, separation, and limitation of the first idea. Herein consists the difference between the conception of bodies and of their actions in former times and at the present day. I shall hereafter have an opportunity of showing that in the discovery of the facts which were accumulated on the original idea of air, and which gradually enlarged and determined its signification, the conception of the new facts preceded their elicitation, - that is, they were *thought* before, and were afterwards discovered by means of experiments based on the idea of their existence.

We can easily perceive that most of our ideas on philosophy, and particularly on jurisprudence, have been discovered and developed in quite a similar manner; that our present conceptions of the words « State » or « Church, » for instance, are quite different to what they were a hundred years ago. Our conception of God changes, purifies, and becomes enlarged with our idea of « force. »

In the course of the development of scientific ideas, each one is of value, inasmuch as it coincides and is bound up with the experiences of the time, so as to make them useful to the mind in developing its methods of thought. The question as to the correctness of the conception is considered later, when it often happens that some of the ideas, which, at an earlier period, had been accounted the most necessary and important, entirely disappear, and are replaced by others, which again, after a time, share the fate of their predecessors. The idea of an elemental FIRE was replaced by that of « SULPHUR; » the theory of « PHLOGISTON » succeeded that of sulphur; it was then thought that fire was caused by OXYGEN, and now we believe that light and heat, as displayed in it, are the consequence of CHEMICAL ACTION and other natural forces.

Each of our present conceptions is the fruit of time, of infinite work and mental exertion ; hence, if our speculations are less bold than those of the Greeks, it is their example which has taught us that the highest flights of the imagination, with the most subtle logic, cannot alter our position with regard to science, and that they cannot change or expedite the regular course of the development of ideas founded on experience. Euclid, with his powerful mathematical mind, believed that sight was dependent upon visual rays passing out from the eyes ; and Descartes, one of the greatest thinkers of any age, could not raise his mind to the conception of an attractive force. Our present conception that gravity is innate, inherent, and essential to matter, apppeared to Newton as so great an absurdity, that « he could not believe it possible for any man, who in philosophical matters had an average power of thinking, to fall into such an error ; » and in rejecting the Newtonian doctrine that the heavenly bodies are moved by the composition of a centripetal with an original projectile force, the great Leibnitz said that God could not make a body revolve round a distant centre, unless by some impelling mechanism or by a miracle, « *qu'il mit un ange à ses trousses.* » [1]

It is a very general opinion that there exists a gap between the cessation of scientific inquiries amongst the Greeks and their recommencement, in the fifteenth century ; thus it is that the Middle Ages are described by historians as a period of stagnation, and the fifteenth century as one of a re-awakening of science.

This view, as regards Europe, is only partially

correct, and cannot apply to Germany, England, and what is now called France, in which Grecian and Roman learning could not have been extinguished in the Middle Ages, as it was only introduced into these countries at a much later period. We must take into consideration that at the time when learning was at its maximum in Athens, Western Europe was inhabited by half-savage tribes, whose only dress was the skins of wild beasts. In the time of Charlemagne, the chief state officials and the most powerful barons could not write their own names. We must remember that even in the thirteenth century, Rome was the centre of commerce for Christian slaves, while at Lyons and in the sea-coast towns of the Baltic and the German Ocean large slave-markets were held.

The endeavours of the great Emperor to educate the rude and ignorant clergy of his time, by founding schools, were without effect, because at that period civilisation had not prepared the ground for cultivation. The extension of mental culture in a nation depends upon the increase of inventions amongst the people, that is, upon its advance in civilisation. Through such inventions new facts are won from nature, and these facts are necessary for the increase of conceptions founded on experience as materials for thought.

As mental culture is the mother of science, there is still a further condition necessary for its development. It is dependent upon the establishment of a class of men who occupy themselves with the education of the mind, to the exclusion of every other object. But the men who devote themselves to this task do not produce anything which they can exchange in the market for the necessaries of life ; hence such a class cannot exist until the population has amassed a certain superfluity of riches beyond those required by their possessors to satisfy their material necessities. As soon as they are in this position the wants of intellect are felt, and the rich classes expend a portion of their wealth on the means of cultivating their minds.

Although there was uninterrupted communication between the Eastern Empire and Italy in the Middle Ages, and no impediments existed to prevent the extension of Byzantine learning, its entrance into the western countries did not take place until the fourteenth century, because the intellectual classes had not yet arisen in them, and, therefore, the conditions for its nurture and further development were still wanting. It is unnecessary to say that Grecian cultivation in Western Europe could only advance in proportion as the people approached the civilisation of antiquity.

It can easily be shown that the civilisation of the European nations has steadily advanced since the downfall of the ancient Greek States, although, from peculiar circumstances which I shall soon touch upon, it for a time without influence on the advance of mental culture in Western Europe. Hence there is an apparent gap in the progress of science.

We have now reached the point where we propose to direct attention to the share which inventions have in developing the conceptions or ideas of natural science. For example, the true view of the movement of the earth and of the planets dates from the discovery of the telescope, as all advances in astronomy were dependent upon the improvement of optical instruments. The invention of the telescope preceded that of colourless glass. All further improvements in optical instruments depended upon the invention of flint-glass, and of achromatic lenses, which Newton thought to be impossible. With Galileo's instruments the discovery of Uranus and the planets of Saturn would never have been made. Copernicus did not think that his own views were « true. » He only looked upon them as more « simple » and « beautiful » than those which preceded, - just as we look upon the ideas of a psychologist as « good and beautiful, » as « adequate, » « profound, » and « complete, » without considering them true in the same sense that two and two make four.

Chemical analysis is derived from testing metals; mineral chemistry from pharmacy, and from the manufacture of chemicals ; while organic chemistry proceeds from medicine.

The laws of heat have been extended by the invention of the steamengine ; those of light by photography.

In astronomy, the Greeks accomplished the utmost

that they possibly could with the aid of one single sense. They discovered the laws of the reflection of light, the arithmetical laws of sound, the centre of gravity, the principles of the lever as well as of hydrostatic pressure ; and they found all that could be developed out of these laws by the help of mathematics and astronomical observations. But further advancement was limited by the degree of their civilisation.

The source of the wealth, trade, and power of the Grecian States, when they were in their prime, was a highly developed, widely-spread industry. Corinth produced what we might call Birmingham and Sheffield wares, Athens was the centre of the manufactures which we now find divided between Leeds, Staffordshire, and London, - such as woollen cloths, dyes, pottery, gold and silver utensils, and shipbuilding. The citizens were manufacturers on the largest scale, shipowners and merchants who had their offices and factories along the. whole coasts of the Black Sea and the Mediterranean ; the men of science were the sons of citizens, and thus became familiar with trade, manufacture, and commerce. Thales was a trader in oil; Socrates was a stonemason ; Aristotle an apothecary ; Plato and Solon were not strangers to trade.

In ancient Greece, the learned man spoke the same language. as the tradesman. The mind of the latter had been as highly cultivated as that of the philosopher, the difference between them consisting only in the direction of their knowledge. Democratic institutions united them in an intimate personal intercourse. In fact, the thirty-eight chapters of « Problems » do not appear to be anything else than a series of questions from tradesmen, artists, musicians, architects, and engineers, which Aristotle endeavoured to solve as far as his conceptions, founded on the experience then existing, enabled him to do.

Until the time of Pericles, no other country of the ancient world united the necessary conditions for the rise of science as they were found in Greece, owing to its social state and to the intimate that existed between the productive and intellectual classes. But Greece was a slave State, and in slavery lay the ban which contracted its civilisation within fixed limits that could not be extended.

All the products of Grecian manufacture were the fruits of slave labour. When Athens was in her prime, every 100 citizens possessed nearly 2000 slaves, a number which gives an idea of the extraordinary development of Athenian industry.

It is clear that as an artisan or mechanic is not able to produce more than is actually necessary for the subsistence of himself and his family, he must have the strength of twenty or more men at his disposal, if he is to obtain a surplus of the products of his industry large enough to satisfy the wants of a portion of the population of the country in which he lives ; and all the artisans in the country must produce a still larger surplus before they can carry on an export-trade. This last condition exists in all manufacturing nations, and also existed in Greece. The wealth that accumulated there in precious metals was not the fruit of depredation, but had been gained by the exchange of their industrial products with the people of other countries, to whom these manufactures were more valuable than gold and silver.

The further progress of Grecian civilisation depended essentially on its passage from a slave-state into a free-state; but the existence of the latter is only conceivable by the use of natural powers, which, through the aid of machinery, enable the work of the slaves to be performed.

It is clear that the invention of a machine which changes a given natural force, such as that of falling water, into a mechanical power capable of doing the work of twenty men, opens to the inventor a source of wealth, and enables the slaves to be set free who were formerly employed in the labour ; thus the natural consequence of the introduction of machines is to augment the class of producers as well as that of inventors, and at the same time to increase the general productiveness of the country. But in a slave-state the application of natural power is practically impossible, as the profits and riches of the wealthy classes depend on the slaves, so that every individual citizen looks upon the introduction of machinery as an actual menace to his property. When the citizens not only hold slaves, but are also at the same time the source of political power, the government and the people unite in order to render slavery permanent. The government thus acts with the apparent object of insuring the means of subsistence to the working population.

The free man alone and not the slave has a natural impulse to improve and invent new tools, and an interest in doing so; for we generally see that the workmen who are engaged in putting together a newly-invented machine become joint-discoverers, by finding out something to render it more complete.. The doctor and the regulator, which belong to the most important parts of the steam-engine, were the inventions of workmen.

Slaves, who are themselves merely machines, do not invent machines or new methods of manufacture.

Liberty alone loosens the fetters which prevent man employing to the best advantage the powers lent him by God ; it is the most important of all the conditions for the advancement of mankind in civilisation and mental culture.

A glance at China suffices to show us the influence produced upon a gifted people by shutting them out from the employment of natural force, through the agency of machinery, for the performance of human labour. Its high civilisation has from this cause been rendered stationary for two thousand years.

In England, and particularly in the United States of

America, where antiquated State-regulations and laws, the offspring of ignorance, do not check the free employment of man's faculties, we see a constant increase in wealth, power, and civilisation ; and one can hardly entertain a doubt, that in the population of the free States of North America all the conditions are present that are necessary to enable them to reach the highest pinnacle of mental culture attainable by man.

A modern State, in which free-trade does not exist, where the prosecution and extension of a business are dependent on the ignorant will of officials ; where the free man is prevented from choosing the place which he considers most suitable for the employment of his faculties ; and where he must obtain the permission of his master before he can marry, - this is like the slave-state of antiquity, where the bulk of the people are poor and insusceptible of either mental or moral culture, and where wealth and power form a thin varnish, which the slightest friction will remove.

We see the effect of riches on the mind of the productive classes in commercial countries, where trade has sprung out of industry. The sons of prosperous manufacturers and merchants turn away from their father's occupations, although they were the source of their own riches. Their aim is not the acquirement of wealth, for of that they have already a superfluity ; but they desire honour and consideration, and devote themselves to Science, or to the service of the State, the Army, or the Church. In this manner the intellectual classes spring out of the productive classes.

In modern Europe a manufactory rarely descends to the third generation, while most mercantile houses pass into other hands in the second. Upon this depends the renewal of the whole industrial population with every generation, and the constant infusion of new life into industry. The manufacturers, who have enriched themselves, make room for those who are ascending the ladder of industry by means of new inventions, and a circulation is thus started in the country, by which its power and riches are constantly increasing.

In Greece the relations that existed were quite of a different nature. There, as everywhere, wealth produced the intellectual classes, whose subsistence must be insured by the productive classes ; but the latter were not renewed or invigorated in Greece. The freeman who had no fortune was obliged to emigrate; he might invent a machine, but he could not invent slaves, and without them the road to wealth by means of industry was blocked up in his country, and that of commerce only was open to a limited number.

A free circulation is the main support of industry and of productive power in a population; all progress depends on its existence; when it ceased in the Grecian States they had reached the limits of their civilisation and culture. The enriched people produced no new inventions, and, when no more facts were elicited from nature, the source of the enlargement of mental power was exhausted ; that is to say, as there was no increased growth of ideas derived from experience, there could be no further advancement of culture, for which these were indispensable.

The internal trade of Greece must have gradually interchanged its products, in an export trade, with those of other lands; and this enabled the accumulated capital to be retained some time longer, but the life-blood of the slave-state was dried up hundreds of years before the time when its fall was proclaimed by external signs.

The civilisation of the Greeks passed through the Roman Empire and the Arabs into all the countries of Europe, and its continued further development, through the whole of the Middle Ages, is evident in the increase of inventions. Towards the end of the fifteenth century we already find a systematic algebra and trigonometry, the mode of reckoning by decimals, an improved calendar, and the foundations laid for a thorough revolution in the department of medicine. We find wonderful improvements in the processes of mining and smelting, in dyeing, weaving, tanning, and the manufacture of glass, in engineering and architecture, and particularly in the province of chemistry. Paper, telescopes, guns, watches, the art of knitting with needles, table-forks, horse-shoes, bells, chimneys and flues, wire-drawing machines, the manufacture of steel, the art of engraving on wood aud copper, and glass for the table, were discovered; mirrors made of glass backed with an amalgam of mercury and tin, wind-mills and saw-mills, were invented, while corn-mills and looms were improved.

These inventions give an idea of the advancement of civilisation in Western Europe, the progress of mental culture in the fifteenth century being intimately associated with them and with the geographical discoveries which took place about the same time.

We find a flourishing trade, embracing all Europe, extending from Genoa, Pisa, and Venice, to the coast towns of the North Sea and the Baltic, thus uniting it with the East, Arabia, and the Indies. The basis of this commerce is an industry of great extent in the manufacturing towns of the Netherlands, Italy, Germany, and England. We see arising in these countries a free and prosperous middle class, and out of it, as the natural consequence of accumulated wealth, the intellectual classes are formed. The further growth of Grecian and Roman began from this period.

When the learned classes first arose, all their powers were for some time expended in endeavouring to take possession of the inheritance of mental treasures which had descended to them from antiquity. As long as they had to learn, and were still scholars, Grecian and Roman did not revive in them so as to produce further development, and they could not really fulfil their calling as teachers of the people. They turned away, and not without reason, from the people and their language, as the literature of their own country hardly offered them anything that was worthy of attracting or captivating minds filled with the models of antiquity.

The position and occupation of the learned men in that time combined to exclude them from communication with the productive classes, and so the literature of this period does not unfold the degree of civilisation and mental culture amongst the people. The knowledge which circulated among them, and impressed itself on their thoughts, had been derived from their closer contact with physical laws, and increased in proportion to the amount of more correct conceptions formed by them of the nature of bodies and of their mutual relations. But as this knowledge was not yet gathered up and recorded in books, it did not come under the notice of the learned class.

This separation of the learned men scarcely retarded the approach of the intellectual and productive classes, because, until the fourteenth century, the followers of trade and industry did not possess the necessary means to bring that approximation about, owing to the unformed state of their book language. The so-called singer guilds, working successfully in singing-schools amongst the citizens, took the place of the learned men in developing and enlarging the language, both in words and in writing. Until then the productive classes had been directed in the exchange and the increase of knowledge by personal intercourse in travelling ; they were wandering classes of society, but, with the acquisition of a book language, the facts and knowledge that they had gained were collected and spread abroad. The arts of writing and reading, which had been hitherto unknown to the operatives, were felt to be the most important means of increasing and disseminating knowledge among the people. Their value was first perceived in the industrial towns, where a wandering life was incompatible with the habits of business. In these cities the first public schools were founded.

The impulse to extend the knowledge of the ancients by means of schools was as strong amongst the learned classes as was the eagerness for information amongst the operatives. Both circumstances stimulated the demand for books, and it was the difficulty of satisfying this want by copying manuscripts that called forth the discovery of printing in the middle of the fifteenth century. A century earlier this would have had no influence on mental development; but from the time of its occurrence, we date a new period in the history of mental culture.

If we glance over the literature towards the end of the century in which the first book was printed, we are filled with astonishment at the extent and importance of the achievements in natural science and medicine, and at the extraordinary mass of facts and knowledge in astronomy, engineering, manufactures, and trades, which had been gained and handed to posterity by the people of the Middle Ages. This knowledge had been collected by the medical men, who were educated at the schools of learning, and who stood next in social position to the productive classes. In the sixteenth century, medical men were the founders of modern science ; they took part in the increase and extension of Grecian knowledge.

Another century and a half, however, passed away, before the knowledge collected and gained by them had been systematically arranged, and was sufficiently extensive and complete, to become effectual as a means of instruction in the schools and universities. Until that time the foreign language in which this mass of information had been recorded was familiar to all the learned in Europe ; and it therefore possessed the inestimable advantage of uniting the men of every country who devoted their powers to the building up of science by solving her great problems. Had the Latin language not been general this powerful co-operation would have been impossible. Towards the end of the eighteenth century, when the vernacular was introduced into schools and general literature, the last barrier fell which had divided the intellectual from the productive classes ; both again, as in ancient Greece, spoke the same language, and understood one another; then science, learning, and poetry cooperated with the aim of spreading mental in an equally high degree through all classes.

With the extinction of the slavery of the past, and with the combination of ALL the conditions for the further development of the human mind, civilisation and mental culture made advances which will prove infinite, indestructible, and imperishable.

A change ensued as science advanced in its natural development. For a long period it had depended for its facts on metallurgists, apothecaries, and manufacturers generally, and had converted the facts thus amassed into rational conceptions, which were now returned to the productive classes in the form of explanations capable of being realized by them in the exercise of their calling.

The antipathy of the practical classes to theory now passed away ; the artisan, the manufacturer, the farmer, again applied, as in ancient Greece, to the theorist for advice.

Another change took place when the learned and scientific as well as teachers of medicine, acquired the technical skill and dexterity of the practical classes, and when the latter adopted the firmly established laws and the principles of science which had been discovered by the learned.

Thus, in pursuing their different objects, the scientific man became an independent inventor, while the manufacturer, the artisan, and the farmer became independent inquirers, and, in an intellectual sense, freemen.

Our glance into the future displays a scene of incessant and productive activity.

The past now appears to us in another light. We look upon the conflict of the scholars and divines with scientific inquirers in the Middle Ages, as an occurrence of no importance ; it arose from their inability to draw a distinction between a dogma and a fact. The combined spiritual and temporal power could not prevent the inventions of the telescope or the compass, or the discovery of oxygen ; nor could it suppress the effects of this acquired knowledge on the minds of the people. It is possible to burn books, but not facts.

When it was proved that the earth is a small planet which revolves round the sun, the earlier conception of

HEAVEN was modified ; and with the explanation of fire, the idea as to the nature of HELL altered also. As soon as the pressure of air was discovered, witchery and sorcery were no longer tenable, for with it nature lost her « ABHORRENCE of a vacuum, » and her VOLITION, her LOVE, and her HATRED passed away. With these discoveries man began to feel his strength and his real position in the universe.

With reference to scholastic philosophy, even if Aristotle and Plato had arisen from their graves as teachers in the schools of the Middle Ages, they could not have promoted knowledge, owing to the want of new ideas gathered from experience. The logic of the scholars, and the metaphysics based on it, served best for their own time and that of the future ; but their hostile attitude toward later scientific inquiries was wholly ineffectual.

If science had allied itself with the whole power of

Church and State, it would not have advanced one step further than it has done, neither would it have been developed earlier or in any other way.

We know now that the ideas of men are organically developed according to fixed laws of nature and of the human mind. We see the tree of knowledge which the Greeks planted in the soil of civilisation growing up and developing without interruption, blooming and bearing fruit at the appointed time in the sunshine of freedom. We have learnt that its brunches can be bent by external power, but that they can never be broken ; while its countless and delicate roots lie so deeply concealed that it is enabled to pursue its silent growth entirely withdrawn from the arbitrary will of man.

The history of nations informs us of the useless endeavours of political and ecclesiastical power to retain men either in bodily or mental slavery.

Future history will describe the victories of freedom gained by men in their inquiries into the real nature of things, and of truth, - victories with weapons unstained by blood, and won in battles in which morality and religion will range themselves as zealous allies on the side of advancement and science.

***

NOTE

1- « *qu'il mit un ange à ses trousses.* » ; he put an angel after him.

***

Nielrow Editions
frwor@outlook.com

Louis Braille : *The 1839 brochure* (english)
Louis Braille : *Nouveau procédé pour représenter par des points... (Brochure de 1839)*
Charles Suisse : *Restauration du château de Dijon*
Victor Coissac : *La conquête de l'espace*
J.O.B. : *Les épées de France*
Casimir Coquilhat : *Trajectoires des fusées volantes*
Implex : *Mots croisés ; 49 défis*
Arnold Netter : *De l'argent colloïdal*
Robert de Launay : *La question des effectifs à Alésia*
Jean-Baptiste Savigny : *Radeau de la Méduse*
Beaumarchais : *Essai sur le genre dramatique*
Pierre Louis de Maupertuis : *Voyage en Laponie*
Dr Wiart : *De l'usage interne de l'eau de mer*
Corneille de Nélis : *La pierre Brunehaut*
Abbé Mann : *Dissertation sur les déluges*
John Law : *The company of Mississipi* (english/french)
Pierre-Adolphe Piorry : *Sur le danger de la lecture des livres de médecine*
Albert de Lacouperie:*The Miryeks of Korea* (english/french)
Nielrow, collectif : *Makandal, rebelle des Antilles*
Erwin Lo : *Histoires du pays des francons*
Jeremy Bentham : *Emancipate your colonies* (english/french)
Léon Foucault : *Mémoire de 1851 et autres textes*
Jean Couturier : *Mémoire sur l'instruction publique*
Ernest Champeaux : *Cimetières et marchés du vieux Dijon*
Julius Liebig : *The development of science among nations* (english)

Dijon

Dépôt légal mars 2020